5/90

OUTSTANDING AMERICAN BONSAI

A display of extra small or "Shohin" size bonsai and accent plants on display at the 1987 International Bonsai Congress in Minneapolis.

OUTSTANDING AMERICAN BONSAI

A Photographic Essay
On The Works Of Fifty American Bonsai Artists

Written and Edited
by
Randy T. Clark

Photography
by
Peter Voynovich

TIMBER PRESS
Portland, Oregon

The front jacket photo is of a Dwarf Hinoki Cypress (*Chamae-cyparis obtusa* 'Nana') designed by the author. The tree is approximately 28 years old and has been in training as a bonsai for six years. It stands 16 inches high and is planted in a blue-green glazed container of Japanese manufacture. This Hinoki was used as the "logo" tree for the 1987 International Bonsai Congress.

The back jacket photo is of a Japanese Garden Juniper (*Juniperus procumbens*). It is approximately 35 years old, stands 15 inches tall, and is planted in an oval, unglazed brown container with a dragon motif. The tree was designed by the author.

© 1989 by Timber Press, Inc.
All rights reserved

ISBN 0-88192-134-3
Printed in Hong Kong

TIMBER PRESS, INC.
9999 SW Wilshire
Portland, Oregon 97225

Library of Congress Cataloging-in-Publication Data

Clark, Randy T.
    Outstanding American bonsai : a photographic essay on the works of
fifty American bonsai artists / written and edited by Randy T. Clark
; photography by Peter Voynovich.
        p.   cm.
    Includes indexes.
    ISBN (invalid) 0-88192-134-2
    1. Bonsai. 2. Bonsai--Pictorial works. I. Voynovich, Peter.
II. Title.
SB433.5.C62   1989
635.9'772--dc19
                                                    88-37069
                                                      CIP

CONTENTS

To Ralph and Betty
With Love

Japanese Black Pine by Mas Imazumi of California. See additional photo and editor's note on page 73.

STRONG TIMBER

The tree that never had to fight
For sun and air and light,
That stood out on the open plain,
And always got its share of rain,
Never became a forest king,
But lived and died a scrubby thing.

The man who never had to toil,
Who never had to win his share,
Of sun and sky and light and air,
Never became a manly man,
But lived and died as he began.

Good timber does not grow in ease,
The stronger wind . . . the tougher trees,
The farther sky . . . the greater length,
The more the storm . . . the more the strength.

By sun and cold; by rain and snows;
In tree or man, good timber grows,
Where thickest stands the forest growth,
We find the patriarchs of both.

And they all converse with the stars,
Whose broken branches show the scars,
Of many winds and much of strife,
This is the common law of life.

                  Author Unknown

A Rosemary styled as a literati or bunjin bonsai by Buffy Delaney of Minnesota.

A Tamarack or Easter Larch bonsai designed by Don Ganglehoff of Minnesota.

FOREWORD

I often wonder how I managed to get myself mired hip deep in the wonderful world of teeny tiny trees. Today, my garden is filled with hundreds of bonsai. A glance at the calendar reveals a myriad of meetings, workshops, conventions, classes, and other activities all related, in some way, to my involvement with this strange, unconventional and all-consuming hobby. When the phone rings or the mail arrives, it is more often than not a request for advice on a sick plant or an invitation to talk about bonsai. In slightly more than a decade I have been transformed from a typical, middle-class American with only a passing interest in things horticultural, into a chronic and compulsive tree trimmer.

It was not always so. Almost 20 years ago when it all began, there were no meetings and no trees. Because I was planted firmly in the heartland of the great American Midwest, information on the subject was virtually unavailable. True, bonsai was well and indeed thriving in places such as southern California with its large Japanese and Chinese American populations, but in the corn fields of Iowa and Minnesota bonsai was almost unknown.

How then did a guy who prefers cheeseburgers to sushi and beer to sake ever develop such a fervent concern for root buttresses, faulty apexes and good trunk taper? Perhaps this book will help to answer that question. In the following pages the reader will find many words, but more importantly dozens of illustrations representing the best efforts of 50 outstanding American bonsai artists.

The illustrations are the real reason for this book and true key to the meaning and purpose of bonsai. They need no words; bonsai speak quietly, but eloquently for themselves. They are a distillation of nature's beauty, elegance and peace. They are an affirmation that after corporate boardrooms, tax audits, oil spills, terrorist bombings and AIDS, life still exists, still is simple and in that simplicity is a thing of overwhelming beauty.

The grandeur of the Rocky Mountains can be captured in a 10-inch container. The forests of the Appalachians, the desert of the Mojave, the canyons of Arizona, the lakes, plains and valleys of North America can be captured alive and brought home for everyone to experience.

I hope the reader enjoys this book. I only wish there were some way to include all of the many outstanding American artists whose work deserves inclusion here. U.S. and Canadian interest in bonsai grows wider each day. We have not been at it for as long as our friends and teachers living on that small island half a world away, but we are pursuing our new love with a passion. And, like most things Americans set out to do, we are getting pretty good at it, as the photographs on the following pages will attest.

For years North Americans have looked at lavishly illustrated Japanese books depicting the best in bonsai half a world away. For most of us, looking was all we could do since they were written in kanji, with measurements in metric. Here then is an English language book, with measurements in good old feet and inches and depicting some of the best we have to offer. I wrote it for us and I wrote it as kind of a report card to our teachers with the thought that someday, in the not-too-distant future, the teacher may be able to learn something from the student.

Randy Clark
Minneapolis 1989

ACKNOWLEDGMENTS

Many of the bonsai in this book were created by friends, and a good many more by people I have never met. All are talented artists, and I thank them for allowing me to depict and comment upon their work here. I also wish to thank the National Bonsai Foundation, for without their exhibit this book would never have come to pass. Thanks are due Bonsai Clubs International and the Minnesota Bonsai Society for permitting me to photograph the trees in the exhibit as well. Above all I wish to thank bonsai artist and photographer Peter Voynovich whose excellent photographs are the backbone of this book. Also a special thanks to Art Cook, Bruce Baker and Tom Kedrok who assisted Peter in the photo sessions. Thanks also to photographers Peter Wong of Minneapolis, Daymon J. Hartley of Detroit and Dr. Carlos Rojas of Florida, as well as Don Gangelhoff and Dr. and Mrs. Roland Hofmeister of Minneapolis for providing the additional images needed to complete the book. Finally I would like to thank my wife Nancy. Her diligent help with the dictionary and her gentle reminders to "get to work" took me away from my bonsai more than I would have liked, but also led this book to be produced much sooner than would have been otherwise possible.

BONSAI IN NORTH AMERICA

The ancient oriental philosopher must have had bonsai in mind when he observed that "One picture is worth a thousand words." The fact is, even the excellent photographs which grace the pages of this book often fail to capture the drama and excitement experienced when seeing bonsai close up and in person for the first time.

The term "American Bonsai" can be a little confusing for those becoming acquainted with the art. As a society, North Americans have been conditioned to think of bonsai as a Japanese art form. This view is not really adequate. Although the beginnings of bonsai are firmly rooted in the Orient, like any art form, it is amenable to adaptation, change and intrepertation to reflect American values and concepts of beauty.

Bonsai literally translated means "to plant in a container." Such a definition might lead the reader to think of bonsai as simply another form of horticulture. Certainly growing bonsai requires a green thumb, but anyone viewing a truly outstanding bonsai recognizes that something more is involved than water, sunshine and fertilizer.

Horticultural principles developed over many hundreds of years play a key role in the maintenance of bonsai, but at its heart, bonsai is an art form requiring the discipline of every art coupled with a clear understanding of line, form, shape, and proportion. The creative principles which artists consider the "tools of the trade" are as necessary in bonsai as they are in painting or pottery. Just as the guiding hand of the sculptor gives meaning and life to the raw clay and stone in which he works, the bonsai artist uses living plant material to create a personal vision. As with any work of art, the finished object is conceived to be seen by others and to stimulate an intellectual or emotional response from the viewer.

North Americans have for some years enjoyed a resurgence of interest in things Oriental. We cook in woks, eat with chop sticks and even relish raw fish and sushi bars. However, when it comes to the ancient, mystical, Oriental art of bonsai, we become a little apprehensive. We reason that such exquisite visions of beauty can only be realized by those with a thorough schooling in the philosophy of Zen Buddhism, and even then only after years of extensive study.

Nothing could be further from the truth. Bonsai is certainly ancient, but there is no mystery, and by any modern definition it is no longer exclusively an Oriental art form. Thousands of North Americans work with bonsai each day. How did bonsai arrive in the land of fast food and rock and roll? The roots of all bonsai (no pun intended) actually began in China and not Japan. Chinese paintings depicting bonsai (Penjing in China) have been found as early as the Sung Dynasty (960–1280 AD), although the practice may have begun much earlier. Penjing were probably introduced

15

into Japan at about the same time as the Buddhist religion in the 6th century. We do know that references to bonsai were made in the records of the Kasuga shrine during the Kamakura period (1192–1333 AD). Small trees in containers also appear in scroll paintings from the same period.

Because of the large number of Japanese and Chinese Americans living on both coasts, the art form has been known in North America for some time. However, because these ethnic communities tended to keep to themselves, a wider knowledge of bonsai did not begin to enter the mainstream of North American life until after World War II. It was then that military personnel stationed in Japan as part of the occupation army were exposed to a variety of Japanese arts and customs, among them bonsai. When they returned home they brought with them a better understanding of the art, and in some cases, a desire to try their hand at it.

Japanese communities in the U.S. and Canada began to share their knowledge of bonsai. Questions were asked, clubs were formed, books were both written and translated, and so today the bonsai community in North America is estimated to number about 10,000 although the actual number could be much larger. At least two major conventions are held each year for English-speaking bonsai growers in various U.S. and Canadian cities, and more than 130 bonsai clubs and societies in 32 states hold regular meetings to teach and study the art.

This explosive growth has not been limited to the U.S. and Canada. Active bonsai organizations have developed in a host of other countries as interest in the art spread. Growers in England, West Germany, India, Italy, Colombia, South Africa and Mexico all participate actively in the international bonsai community. Those in each country work with the plant materials available in their particular region, and although all create bonsai using time honored rules laid down by the Japanese, each brings a unique and particular artistic approach to their trees.

It has been suggested it is not possible for North Americans to practice "Japanese Bonsai." The artist's objective in bonsai is to create his or her vision of beauty by working with the available plant material. In the motion picture *Karate Kid* the venerable Japanese master tells his young student to close his eyes and picture a tree. He then hands him clippers, points to the raw plant material on the table and says, "Now, make look like picture."

The trees pictured in the teacher's mind are those which grow on the slopes of Mount Fuji. The student however, raised in the heartland of America, envisions trees growing upon the slopes of the Rocky Mountains or the Sierra Nevada. Each of us is a product of our cultural heritage and so will interpret our world through that heritage. When making our bonsai, each cuts and prunes using what skills are possessed, but to the visions and images accumulated over a lifetime. This is the real excitement and challenge of bonsai: not to emulate what our Japanese teachers have given us, but to honor those teachings by bringing a new way of seeing to this ancient art.

THE NATIONAL BONSAI FOUNDATION EXHIBITION

This book is based on illustrations of the work of 50 outstanding American bonsai artists. The logistics of producing such a publication were considerable. Obtaining high quality, uniform photographs of bonsai by artists scattered across North America could have been a complex and expensive undertaking had it not been for The National Bonsai Foundation.

The National Bonsai Foundation is a very special organization devoted to excellence in American bonsai. Its primary objective has been and remains the development of funding for construction of a complex of buildings to house North American and Chinese bonsai on the grounds of the U.S. National Arboretum in Washington D.C.

In July 1987 the Foundation sponsored an exhibition entitled *Outstanding American Bonsai.* This exhibit was produced for the Foundation by the Minnesota Bonsai Society and Bonsai Clubs International, as a part of the 1987 International Bonsai Congress, held in Minneapolis that year.

It was the first time an exhibit of world class bonsai, created by artists designated among the best in the United States, had ever been assembled in one place. The exhibit was a landmark in the history of American bonsai and a unique photographic opportunity.

About a year prior to the Congress, the National Bonsai Foundation asked its directors throughout the country to provide the names of those individuals in their regions whom they felt ranked among the best in American bonsai. More than 100 individuals were nominated. Each nominee was then invited to display one selection of his or her work in this special exhibition.

The logistics and costs of transporting a valuable bonsai across a great distance are considerable. The exhibit was to be produced at no cost to the Foundation, which meant that all expenses and risk had to be borne by the artists themselves. Despite these hurdles, more than 50 artists agreed to provide a tree for the exhibition, and the result was an event unique in the annals of American bonsai. More than 4000 people viewed the exhibit during its five-day stay in Minneapolis.

Through Foundation sponsorship of the exhibit in Minneapolis, and with the cooperation of Bonsai Clubs International and a great deal of hard work by the Minnesota Bonsai Society, the exhibit became a reality.

The illustrations on the following pages are almost entirely of bonsai displayed in the National Bonsai Foundation Exhibition. Three or four have been added from other sources to round out the selection. Our only regret is that we are unable to illustrate the works of the many exceptional artists who were unable to bring their bonsai to Minneapolis.

Like the Foundation exhibit, this book is also unique in the history of American bonsai. There are many publications available which deal with the "how to" of bonsai. There are also many picture books showing excellent bonsai from various regions of the country. Most notable among these are those produced yearly by The California Bonsai Society. This publication, however, marks the first time that a representative sampling of the work of bonsai artists from across the United States has been gathered together in a single volume.

American bonsai reflect North American trees and landscapes created by American artists. Like music, bonsai is a common language offering a unique universe into which all may journey. For a moment, a bonsai only inches high may recall a tall windswept pine; a tuft of moss may remind the viewer of the green grass in a meadow. Small stones can suggest mighty mountains and young seedlings, the trees of a great forest.

Those who appreciate bonsai instinctively understand its symbolism. Unlike other art forms, it requires no explanation, but rather offers an instant and intimate communication between subject and viewer. The spirit of bonsai restates our own relationship with nature. As the artist paints on canvas and the sculptor carves in stone, so the bonsai artist uses living plant material to create a reflection of nature in miniature.

The bonsai artist distills nature by shaping trunk, branch and leaf into a statement of elegant simplicity and harmony. In so doing, he reduces nature to a more personal and intimate scale. The bonsai, in its smallness, speaks quietly, but eloquently, of a larger and infinitely more complex universe.

The intention of this book is not so much to teach as it is to inspire. As the reader views the magnificent trees pictured in these pages it should be remembered that bonsai is beauty, and beauty, as we all know, is in the eye of the beholder.

A partial view of the National Bonsai Foundation exhibit at IBC'87 in Minneapolis.

A display of extra small or "Shohin" size bonsai which were a part of the Minnesota Bonsai Society exhibit at IBC '87.

19

A HOME FOR AMERICAN BONSAI

One day, in the not-too-distant future, Americans may be able to visit a place in their nation's capital dedicated to the art of bonsai and to the kinds of magnificent trees pictured in this book. The National Bonsai Foundation is working diligently to provide a permanent home for American bonsai. With the support of individuals and corporations the dream is becoming a reality. The Foundation was formed in 1982. It came into existence because people viewing the Japanese Bonsai Pavilion in Washington D.C. expressed an interest in also seeing examples of American designed bonsai.

The Japanese Gift

In commemoration of the U.S. bicentennial, a rare and priceless gift of 53 bonsai was presented to the American people by the Nippon Bonsai Association. The trees were a gift from the people of Japan. Several of the trees were more than 350 years old and were hand-selected from among the finest bonsai treasures in Japan. The collection included several specimens donated by Japan's Imperial Family as well as a number of leading government and business officials.

The U.S. government, recognizing the significance of this gift, provided funding for a special pavilion to house these priceless treasures. The pavilion was designed by nationally famous architect Masao Kinoshita and located on the grounds of the U.S. National Arboretum in Washington D.C. Each year, for more than a decade, the Japanese Bonsai Pavilion has been seen by thousands of visitors to the nation's capital. Today, the Pavilion and its adjacent Japanese Garden serve as an oasis of peace and beauty within the confines of a busy, major city.

The Foundation

In the early 1980s, Dr. John Creech, then Director of the National Arboretum, noticed many viewing the exhibit of Japanese bonsai ask why no American bonsai were on display. The question was repeated with sufficient frequency that Dr. Creech approached a friend, Mrs. Marion Gyllenswan, about the possibility of erecting some type of structure at the Arboretum to house American bonsai. Mrs. Gyllenswan, a nationally known bonsai instructor, was intrigued by the concept and agreed to explore the idea with her associates in the bonsai community.

The idea took hold and in 1982 the National Bonsai Foundation was formed as a non-profit, tax exempt organization whose purpose was to

A partial view of the interior of the Japanese Bonsai Pavilion in Washington D.C.

solicit funding and oversee the planning, construction and maintenance of an educational facility to be known as *The National Bonsai Complex.* The complex would be built on the Arboretum grounds adjoining the existing Japanese Pavilion.

The key element in the complex was to be a North American Bonsai Pavilion, designed to showcase American trees created by American artists. In addition, the complex called for the incorporation of a Chinese rockery and a special pavilion for Chinese penjing, plus a Japanese tea house, a koi pond, and special areas for temporary displays, educational programs and bonsai maintenance.

At this writing, the National Bonsai Complex remains a dream. But as time passes, support grows. When the project is finally complete it will be a unique complex. For the first time anywhere, including Japan, a facility will exist which offers visitors an opportunity to compare and contrast the various styles of bonsai. The juxtaposition of Japanese, American and Chinese bonsai will provide the means for a study in similarities and differences stimulating from both artistic and horticultural standpoints.

Additional information about the National Bonsai Foundation is available by writing the Foundation's Executive Director at P.O. Box 32377, Washington D.C. 20007.

OUTSTANDING AMERICAN BONSAI

Japanese Garden Juniper
Juniperus procumbens

This exceptional informal, upright bonsai stands more than 42 in. high and is the tallest pictured in this volume. It is one of a small handful of specimens salvaged from the removal of an overgrown foundation planting at D. Hill nursery in Elgin, Illinois. The tree is estimated to be 80–100 years old and has been in training as a bonsai for the past 10 years. It is affectionately referred to as "snake" by its owner and is planted in a square, unglazed, brown container of Japanese manufacture. The movement and mass of the tree suggest the feeling of a forest giant. Careful pinching by the artist has resulted in dense and compact foliage. The trunk line displays good taper and visually fascinating movement accentuated by the use of jin and shari, deadwood, in the lower trunk area.

The Artist: Thomas Tecza

Tom Tecza is a Chicago nurseryman who became involved in bonsai in 1974 when bonsai artist Alex Alexander visited his nursery looking for plant material. He invited Tom to join the Elgin Bonsai Study Group of which Alex was a member and mentor. Tom accepted and has been actively involved with the Midwest Bonsai Society ever since. His collection is small, numbering only about 25 plants collected from the wild or purchased as starter material from Japan. He has received the Best of Show award at the Midwest Bonsai Exposition in Chicago on two occasions. Tom has studied almost exclusively with Mr. Alexander and with Japan's Susumu Nakamura who is a frequent visitor to Chicago. Mr. Tecza's landscape nursery business keeps him very busy, but also accounts in part for his enjoyment of bonsai. "Bonsai is quiet. I am never rushed when I work on a tree. There is no deadline and I'm never expected to complete a tree in a specified amount of time," he said.

Water Elm
Planera aquatica

This informal, upright bonsai was collected from the flood plain of Lake Catahoula in central Louisiana in 1983. It was cut back from a height of 30 in. to about 10 in., and the present fine branching structure was developed in four growing seasons. The bonsai is estimated to be 25 to 50 years old and has been in training for four years. It stands 18 in. high and is planted in a rectangular gray container of Japanese manufacture. The tree displays an excellent root buttress and gradual trunk taper. In addition to its small leaves and interesting bark pattern, this species of tree is particularly desirable as a bonsai because it tends to develop fine branch ramifications in a relatively short period of time.

The Artist: Vaughn L. Banting
Vaughn Banting is one of a new generation of talented bonsai teachers and artists in the U.S. His involvement with bonsai began in his early teens and has grown steadily. Today he is a much sought after instructor and appears frequently as a speaker at national bonsai conferences. "My greatest honor has been to be invited to share what I have learned with others," he said. Mr. Banting's personal collection numbers about 150 trees, including Bald Cypress, Black Pine, Maples, Azaleas, Podocarpus, Water Elm and Hornbeam, plus a great many more in various stages of training. "I am very interested in natural deciduous shapes of trees in the United States, and I feel strongly about the need for each country to design bonsai which reflect that country's trees," he said. Vaughn is the founder of the Greater New Orleans Bonsai Society as well as an active participant in various regional and national bonsai organizations. His wife, Donna, is an equally talented bonsai artist who operates "The Garden Gallery," a commercial bonsai nursery and shop in New Orleans. Vaughn is a professionally trained horticulturist and continues to work in the family's nursery and landscaping business. "Bonsai fills my need for artistic expression," he said, "But it also has many spiritual aspects which are very important to me. It forces me to relax and to be content. You can't hurry. Most importantly, bonsai is a membership in the greatest group of people in the world. Bonsai people are sensitive to nature and that appeals a great deal to me."

Japanese Maple
Acer palmatum

This informal, upright forest planting was purchased by the artist in 1981 as a seven-tree planting designed by another artist. The seven-tree forest was displayed at several Minnesota shows and in 1985 appeared at the Midwest Bonsai Show in Chicago where it was critiqued by Susumu Nakamura, a visiting Japanese bonsai master. Mr. Nakamura suggested the removal of two trees which he considered defective and a rearrangement of the five remaining trees, which was done in the spring of 1986. It was necessary to separate the forest's root mass by sawing it into individual cubes; removing the unwanted trees and then reassembling the remaining trees into the present five-tree forest. Guy wires were used to secure each tree to the artist's growing bench until the planting again became stable. It is a light, airy planting which suggests a pleasant walk through a meadow on a sunny afternoon. The tallest tree in the planting stands 36 in. high and is planted in a shallow oval tray of Japanese manufacture. The bonsai is estimated to be 31 years old and has been in training for 11 years. The plant stand is constructed of solid maple and was handmade by the artist in 1985.

The Artist: **Ken Ellis**
Ken Ellis joined the Minnesota Bonsai Society in 1971, along with the Orchid Society and the African Violet Society. He still maintains an interest in orchids and violets, but bonsai seems to be winning. His collection is modest, containing only about 50 finished specimens plus a number of plants in training including a wide variety of indoor, hardy and semi-hardy material. He is a past president and current officer in the Minnesota club as well as a member of several national bonsai organizations. Ken's involvement with the Society has brought him into contact with numerous American bonsai masters. His trees have repeatedly won awards at both the local and regional level. "I enjoy creating and in helping others to create. I think bonsai is an extension of my professional life as an art teacher and audio visual specialist," he said. Ken teaches bonsai classes for the Minnesota Bonsai Society and is actively involved as an adult education teacher of bonsai in Minneapolis and St. Paul. As a part of their bonsai education, Ken often instructs his students in the techniques of designing and firing handmade bonsai containers.

American Arborvitae
Thuja occidentalis

Like a storm-battered, timberline giant, this bonsai speaks of a centuries-old fight against the elements and its determination to survive despite all mother nature can throw at it. This slant-style bonsai makes extensive use of deadwood and in so doing makes a dramatic statement. The plant material was collected and is estimated to be about 125 years old. It has been in training as bonsai for 16 years. It is planted in a round, brown, unglazed Tokoname ware container and stands almost 15 in. high. Like many outstanding bonsai, its current appearance was not the original plan for the tree. The artist, who was then living in the Washington D.C. area, had planned to sell the tree at an auction in the fall of 1985, but that spring it died back to one branch. It was subsequently restyled and has since survived and come to enjoy living in the artist's new Arizona home.

The Artist: Mary Holmes Bloomer

Mary Bloomer "leapt" into bonsai by being elected assistant chairman of the 1978 International Bonsai Congress. It's been non-stop for her ever since. "Bonsai has been good to me. It has brought me wonderful memories, dear friends and even my husband, whom I met at a bonsai convention." Mary's current collection numbers about 20 trees of mostly collected material. The small size of this collection was due to a move from Washington D.C. to Arizona following her marriage to photographer/bonsaist Peter Bloomer. "I only brought the best with me and even then, only those I felt would thrive well in an arid climate," she said. The Bloomers are now rebuilding their collection. Most of her bonsai are driftwood style with a preference for native, collected material such as Ponderosa Pine, California Juniper, Cliff Rose and Manzanita. "I am fortunate because I have at least three lifetimes full of this material from which to choose," she said. Mary uses the Japanese world "shibui" to describe great bonsai. "It's an indefinable something that combines both grace and strength, beauty and form. It transcends the rules and touches my heart and my imagination as well as my eye," she said. "I love being out in the wild and the hunt; the finding of outstanding material and the challenge of making it survive and watching it grow. I also love the peace that spending an afternoon in the warm, spring sunshine working on my trees brings to me, and perhaps as much as anything, I love the friends that bonsai has brought me."

Redwood
Sequoia sempervirens

This Redwood was collected about 25 years ago by Dan Robinson in northern California. It had been rough trained by him, but has since been completely restyled. Branches were repositioned and the former back of the tree became its new front. It is a particularly noteworthy, formal, upright bonsai measuring 34 in. tall. As with all formal uprights, the critical matters of effective branch placement and silhouette have been given excellent attention by the artist. The tree's root buttress and good trunk taper combine with the sparse yet effective use of dead branches, jin, to create the illusion of a giant Sequoia in miniature. The plant is estimated to be 55 years of age and has been in training for 22 years. It is planted in a brown, oval, unglazed Tokoname ware container.

The Artist: Robbieanna Smith

Robbieanna Smith became involved with bonsai in 1970 as a result of her husband's interest in the subject. Together they practice the art and maintain a joint collection of more than 160 plants at their home near Memphis, Tennessee. Ms. Smith has studied with many American bonsai masters and has made 11 trips to Japan for the sole purpose of studying the collections of Japanese masters and visiting bonsai growing nurseries throughout the country. "Seeing so many good bonsai has given me a more critical eye when it comes to assessing our own personal collection," she said. Robbieanna is a regular participant at most North American bonsai shows and energetically scouts new and unusual plant material in the areas she visits. She is an active participant, officer, board member and worker for numerous local and national bonsai organizations and has gained a reputation for her keen artistic eye, sharp wit, pleasant disposition and boundless southern charm. "When I look at a beautiful bonsai I can feel the strength of character of the artist who created it. My husband and I share this obsession and one of my greatest pleasures is locating new material for us to work on."

Parsley-leaf Hawthorn
Crataegus marshallii

This exceptional five-tree forest is one of the few group plantings included in this book. The varying trunk diameters and placement provide the planting with an excellent feeling of depth. Their arrangement at the left of a long narrow tray provides an asymmetrical balance which is visually stimulating. The trees were collected in 1975 and have been in training for 12 years. Originally they were part of a larger eight-tree forest which suffered frost damage in 1983 and were later rearranged into the present grouping. The largest tree in the group stands 23 in. high. They are planted in a 21-inch-wide, brown, unglazed rectangular tray, 1 ¾ in. deep. Fine branching and dense foliage on these Hawthorns indicate careful attention to pinching and pruning by the artist.

The Artist: **Marian Borchers**
Marian Borchers developed an interest in bonsai at the age of 11 when she saw bonsai master Frank Okamura appear as a guest on the television show "What's My Line." Total involvement did not come until 1970, when she and her husband Mark purchased Young's Bonsai Nursery in Tampa, Florida, and renamed it *The Bonsai Garden.* "I didn't know anything about bonsai at the time, but I had just graduated from college, I needed a job and knew I could at least keep them alive until I learned," she said. Ms. Borchers learned quickly, and today the nursery is one of the largest and best known bonsai centers in the U.S. Marion is a professionally trained horticulturist who received her degree from the University of South Florida. The nursery, located on one acre of ground near Busch Gardens in Tampa, offers an extensive assortment of bonsai and pre-bonsai material plus a full line of tools, containers and other bonsai items. In addition to her regular curriculum of classes at the nursery, Marion is a frequent instructor for bonsai clubs along the entire eastern seaboard and throughout the South. She is an active participant in a number of national and local bonsai organizations and has studied extensively with such masters as John Naka, Cliff Potberg, E. Felton Jones and Yuji Yoshimura. Her personal collection of bonsai includes about 100 specimens of mostly collected material. Indeed, the nursery has gained a reputation for the size and variety of collected material available, including Bald Cypress, Buttonwood, Southern Hornbeam and Trident Maple. "Bonsai makes me feel good. It's very therapeutic . . . an excellent way to focus on something beautiful and forget your problems." "After many years of work, a bonsai will begin to develop a personality of its own. That's what separates really great trees from the average," she said.

Rain Tree
Saman arboreum

This striking, informal upright may be a unique specimen for training as bonsai. It is a native of South America and was grown from seeds sent to the artist by relatives stationed with the U.S. embassy in Brazil. Out of approximately 50 seeds cultivated, this specimen has developed into the most outstanding bonsai. The plant develops compound leaves and bears white flowers, but its most striking characteristic is the growth habit of the trunk and branches which tend to develop in a riblike or crescent fashion which make the tree appear almost flat when viewed from the side. It is a highly unusual selection for bonsai, but the artist has done well with it. The tree is approximately eight years old and has been in training as a bonsai for the past five years. It stands 36 in. high and is planted in an unglazed, brown, rectangular container of Japanese manufacture.

The Artist: Jim Moody

Like many bonsai enthuiasts, Florida's Jim Moody became involved in bonsai because his spouse took up the hobby. "I found what she was doing was exciting and challenging, and eventually I was hooked too," he noted. Mr. Moody's collection includes about 75 trees, mostly of the larger variety and predominately of native plant material. He is a past president of the South Palm Bonsai Club and a member of both the American Bonsai Society and Bonsai Clubs International. He has operated a small bonsai nursery stock business from his home for the past 15 years and is a frequent teacher and lecturer on bonsai throughout Florida.

Dwarf Hinoki Cypress
Chamaecyparis obtusa 'Nana'

This Hinoki was imported from Japan in 1915 with several others. They were mature nursery specimens, but not trained as bonsai, because the importer wished to use them for propagation. They were planted in the ground and cuttings were taken for nearly 50 years. In 1961 the artist purchased this specimen and began training it. The tree is a remarkable informal, upright bonsai which exhibits a massive root buttress and dramatic trunk taper. The creative use of deadwood, jin and shari, on this tree are a trademark of the artist and contribute greatly to the bonsai's overall feeling of strength and age. The tree stands 26 in. high and is planted in a $12 \times 9 \times 4$ in. rectangular container. The Hinoki is estimated to be approximately 85 years old. It is without doubt one of the finest bonsai of this type in the U.S.

The Artist: Daniel Robinson

Dan Robinson of Seattle has had a life-long devotion to the creation and design of beautiful trees. Mr. Robinson is one of the new generation of bonsai teachers and an avid and experienced collector who has travelled extensively throughout the U.S. "bringing them back alive." As a free spirit who relies on his close observation of ancient trees in nature, he has great respect for the Japanese traditions, but leaves room for his own creativity and talents for refinement, in order to capture the magic of American bonsai. His collection of more than 350 specimens ranges from the large to small and is comprised primarily of old collected trees of at least 40 different species. "Bonsai is an opportunity for me to release all of my skills and creativity on a piece of living material, the resulting production manifesting my imagery," he said. The quality of Robinson's material coupled with his skill as an artist and his continual attention to detail and grooming make his collection one of the best in the United States. "A great bonsai is one in which the design excites the viewer with its exultation of age, venerability and naturalness."

Kingsville Boxwood
Buxus microphylla 'Kingsville'

There are nine small Kingsville Boxwoods in this excellent tray landscape. The material was grown from cuttings by the artist and are approximately five years old. The forest is planted in a brown rectangular tray 18 in. wide and stands 8¼ in. from the bottom of the pot to the top of the highest tree. Boxwood is a popular subject among bonsai enthusiasts and the Kingsville variety a special favorite among those who prefer the "shohin" or very small class of bonsai. This particular planting shows the artist's clear understanding of the need for harmony and cooperation between the various elements used to create a "saikei" or forest. Mosses, small ferns and rock have been combined with the trees to create a delightful illusion of trees growing on a rocky hillside. The asymmetrical arrangement of the planting delivers both movement and depth. The selection and placement of stones is one of the dominate features of the forest and yet is sufficiently subdued to avoid conflict with the other elements of the forest and retain the primary focus on the trees.

The Artist: Helen Hasselriis
New York's Helen Hasselriis has been a student of American Bonsai Master Yuji Yoshimura since 1968. Although she makes her living as a professional freelance translator, a considerable amount of her time and energy is devoted to bonsai. Her collection numbers more than 100 bonsai and includes a wide variety of species and styles ranging from 3 to 40 in. in height. She has a special preference for tray landscapes, as her work here clearly indicates, as well as a preference for creating twin and multiple trunk bonsai rather than the single trunk variety. Helen is an active member on both the local and national bonsai scene and served as an officer of the Bonsai Society of Greater New York for four years. In 1985 her bonsai were exhibited at a show for Champion Paper Company in Stanford, Connecticut, and in 1986 at the New York Botanical Garden. "Work on bonsai requires total concentration, shutting out all other distractions. For that reason it is very relaxing, albeit exhausting," she said.

Ponderosa Pine
Pinus ponderosa

This bonsai is one of the largest and probably oldest living specimen in the United States. It is a "shi zen" or natural dwarf specimen found growing at the 14,000 ft. level of the Rocky Mountains near Roosevelt National Forest. Based on core specimens taken from dead trees in the area, this bonsai is estimated at more than 900 years old. The planting is valued at more than half a million dollars and was named "Higurashi-no-matsu" or "Sunset Vision" by the late bonsai artist Bob Kataoka of Denver, Colorado, who was instrumental in its collection and initial styling. This magnificent pine must be seen in person to be truly appreciated. It stands 48 in. high and is planted in a brown 36-inch oval container especially made for it by the Matsushita To-en pottery works in Japan. It was discovered in October 1983, carefully removed and containerized over a one year period. Although it has been in training for only three years it already has the marks of a classic bonsai. It will develop even more beauty and sophistication as its refinement continues through the years.

The Artist: Dick Meleney

Dick Meleney of Denver, Colorado, has been involved with bonsai for more than 35 years. His collection of over 150 bonsai is comprised almost entirely of old twisted, naturally dwarfed conifers indigenous to his beloved Rocky Mountains. These include Ponderosa Pine, Limber Pine, Douglas Fir and many native junipers. In addition to his personal collection, Dick operates the Colorado Dwarf Tree Collecting Company in partnership with bonsai artist Harold Sasaki. The company charters collecting trips for bonsai into the mountains and also sells bonsai stock and supplies. In 1985, he worked with members of his local club to stage a benefit for the National Bonsai Foundation. The group hosted an expedition for 11 bonsai artists which collected over 200 trees in three days time and raised $4000 for the Foundation. "I look upon bonsai as a perfect release from the stress of our high-tech, political lives," he said. "It offers a noncontroversial vehicle toward world understanding and the conservation of natural resources." Meleney is a past president of the Rocky Mountain Bonsai Society and an active member of the national bonsai scene.

Limber Pine
Pinus flexilis

The Limber Pine is sometimes also called a White Pine. It is an excellent subject for bonsai because of its short needle habit. This particular specimen was originally collected in the Rocky Mountains of Colorado by the late Mr. M. Tawara. It was obtained by the artist in 1977 and has been in training as a bonsai for 15 years. The tree is estimated to be 400 years old. It stands 31 in. high and is planted in a brown, unglazed Tokoname ware container. Bold use of deadwood in this bonsai suggests a forest ancient which has died and been replaced by another younger tree of the same species.

The Artist: Harold Sasaki

Harold Sasaki first became involved in bonsai in the mid-1950s while living in Hawaii. Today he resides near Denver, Colorado, and is a two-time president and active participant in the Rocky Mountain Bonsai Society. His personal collection is small, numbering only about 40 plants in finished containers. However, he owns and operates Colorado Bonsai Limited, and is in partnership with fellow mountaineer Dick Meleney in the Colorado Dwarf Tree Collecting Company. The company arranges and stages tree collecting expeditions into the Rockies for out of state bonsai collectors. In 1985 Sasaki was one of a number of Colorado club members who staged a collecting expedition to benefit the National Bonsai Foundation. Sasaki is a recognized teacher of bonsai and has studied with such masters as Harry Hirao, John Naka, Ben Oki and Chase Rosade. In 1986 he was one of the featured speakers at the International Bonsai Congress in Washington, D.C. Sasaki maintains his involvement with bonsai because it "satisfies my inner most sense of what fun should be all about."

Three Leaf Akebia
Akebia trifoliate

Many bonsai are grown for the enjoyment of their fruit or flowers. This Akebia is no exception. It is a cascade style bonsai which measures 20 in., top to bottom of cascade, and is planted in a round, unglazed, brown, Tokoname ware container. The plant is estimated to be about 30 years old. It was cultivated from a seedling and grown in the ground for the first 15 years. Green fruit can be seen in this photo, but when ripe, the Akebia's fruit bears the same deep purple coloring as its flower. To avoid stressing the bonsai, the artist only allows it to bear fruit every second year.

The Artist: Mitsuo Umehara
Mitsuo Umehara of San Mateo, California, was introduced to bonsai as a child growing up in Japan. His involvement with the art is a natural extension of his vocation as a Japanese landscape gardener. His collection numbers more than 300 specimens and reflects more than 28 years of involvement with bonsai. He is an active member of the California bonsai scene and has studied with numerous masters including Masaru Yamaki of Hiroshima. "Bonsai is a mirror of natural art. When you observe a good bonsai it brings back many memories of outdoor experiences. The difference between a good and a great bonsai is an emotional response. A great bonsai should exhibit a peaceful, serene feeling," he said. Umehara teaches bonsai in California and believes that it is common experience of peace and beauty which needs to be shared. "Sharing and teaching bonsai to each other is very important. Through this one shares a peace of the soul and the mind."

Bonsai #13

Japanese Boxwood
Buxus japonica

This excellent, informal, upright bonsai was originally styled in 1981 from overgrown nursery stock. The tree has taken numerous honors at bonsai shows in Minnesota, Chicago and Austin, Texas. The bonsai stands 35 in. high and is estimated to be 40 years old. It has been in training for six years. Its curving trunk line gives the tree a visually pleasing asymmetrical quality. The gradual taper of the trunk is accented by a well proportioned root buttress, giving the tree a strong feeling of stability. Deadwood areas have been used just enough to create a feeling of age without detracting from the plant's interesting bark pattern and vigorous green foliage. The brown, pear-skin oval container enhances the natural curves of the tree.

The Artist: Michael Hansen

Mike Hansen's involvement with bonsai began more than 15 years ago in the cold climates of Minnesota and continues today in the sunshine of his present home in Austin, Texas. His collection includes about 30 finished bonsai with another 200 trees in various stages of training. He is an active participant in both the local and national bonsai scene and currently serves as a Vice President of Bonsai Clubs International and a Regional Director for The National Bonsai Foundation. With his wife, Candy, he founded Midwest Bonsai Pottery and has recently added a small bonsai nursery business. Mike teaches bonsai locally and regionally and has studied with a number of American bonsai masters. "A truly great bonsai must command my attention at first glance and evoke a desire to continue viewing and enjoying its presence. Invariably this is accomplished by skillful execution of the design and by using materials to their best advantage . . . both plant and container." "Bonsai is relaxation and enjoyment," Mike said. "What better environment can man experience than to surround himself with nature's most beautiful objects?"

American Elm
Ulmus americana

Both this tree and Bonsai #14B are by the same artist and fall under a special classification of bonsai known as "shohin." This classification is applied to trees which measure 6 in. or less in height. This particular elm is noteworthy because of its small leaf size. Leaves are usually quite large on this species of elm, and it is to the artist's credit that he has managed to reduce their size so greatly, thus maintaining the overall scale of the planting. The plant is 6 in. high and 5 in. wide. It is planted in a green, glazed, rectangular container. The plant material was collected in about 1979 and has been in training as an informal, upright style bonsai for the past eight years. Its proportion, branch placement and excellent taper make it an outstanding specimen.

Japanese Black Pine
Pinus thunbergii

Also a shohin class bonsai this specimen was obtained as a nursery seedling more than 15 years ago. The pine measures 6 in. high and 8 in. wide. It is planted in a brown, round, unglazed container and is styled as an informal upright bonsai. Black pines also tend to have large needles, which the artist has reduced in size very well.

The Artist: James E. Littleton

Jim Littleton of Louisiana is a passionate plant collector and sculptor who specializes in shohin and mame class bonsai (small and smaller still). He is a man of few words and describes his collection as "not very large." Littleton is a past president of the Greater New Orleans Bonsai Society and has studied with such well known American masters as John Naka, Yuji Yoshimura, Toshio Saburomaru, Chase Rosade, Jim Barrett, Melba Tucker and Ben Oki.

Cryptomeria
Cryptomeria japonica 'Lobbii Nana'

The 13 trees which make up this Cryptomeria Grove or Forest planting were obtained from nursery stock. The largest tree measures 28 in. high and is planted in a brown, unglazed, oval tray approximately 25 in. wide. It was originally styled as a seven tree forest by the late Willodeane Riegel. In 1978 six smaller trees, obtained as cuttings from the larger tree, were added to the planting. The oldest tree in this group is 26 years. It has been in training as a bonsai for 19 years.

The Artist: **Marty Klajnowski**
Martha "Marty" Klajnowski, a native of Pittsburgh, became interested in bonsai more than 15 years ago. She is a retired Air Force Colonel who presently resides in Texas, but developed her interest in bonsai while living in Vacaville, California. Her collection includes more than 60 bonsai with a special interest in azaleas. In addition to being an active member in the Vaca Valley and Golden State bonsai organizations, she is also a director of Bonsai Clubs International. Marty lectures and demonstrates throughout Texas as well as teaching beginning classes near her home. "Bonsai is a living art which in addition to being aesthetically pleasing offers serenity and the challenge of creativity," she said.

Bonsai #16

American Arborvitae
Thuja occidentalis

This bonsai was collected in autumn from a sphagnum bog in Michigan's upper peninsula. It is estimated to be more than 170 years old and has been in training as a bonsai for four years. Like most bog-collected specimens its original trunk base was dead. When collected the plant consisted of two live trunks separated by a rotted central trunk. Both live trunks were apparently branches that had air layered themselves as the original trunk died. It was initially styled in a demonstration for the Ann Arbor Bonsai Society. The tree stands 35 in. high and is planted in an unglazed brown rectangle 19 in. wide.

The Artist: Bruce Baker

Bruce Baker, of Michigan, became aware of bonsai after viewing the collection at Longwood Gardens in Pennsylvania. However, it was not until he joined the Ann Arbor Bonsai Society in 1982 that he became actively involved in the art. His collection includes about 80 specimens most of which are medium to large collected plants. He maintains additional plants in growing beds and collects specimens several times a year. His particular favorites are White Cedars. "Anyone can create a good bonsai with practice and by following the rules," Baker said. "Great bonsai is the expression of an artistic vision through the mastery of horticultural techniques and an unusual diligence in carrying through with them. It is both an artistic and an intellectual challenge. No matter how many times I work with a tree, there is still room to improve it and to learn from it." Mr. Baker is an active participant on both the local and national bonsai scene and has studied with several American masters including his close neighbor Jack Wikle.

54

Kingsville Boxwood
Buxus microphylla 'Kingsville'

This outstanding bonsai was purchased as uncut nursery stock in a 5-gallon growing pot in 1977. It was originally styled in a workshop with bonsai master Keith Scott and in 1980 transferred into its first formal bonsai container. The tree's present rectangular container is made of an unusual yellow clay and was acquired three years ago. Although the artist describes the tree as an informal upright, it could also be classified as a multiple trunk bonsai and as such, is an excellent example. It is difficult to get Kingsvilles to develop effective layering of branches without displaying a "pom pom" effect. This bonsai has accomplished that layering effect well and is reminiscent of the apple and pear orchards from which we used to "snitch" fruit as a child. The planting is estimated to be 65 years old and has been in training for 10 years. It stands 15 in. high and 14 in. wide.

The Artist: Ivan Watters

Ivan Watters of Chicago bought a copy of Yuji Yoshimura's book on bonsai in 1960. Although he had always been interested in plants, it wasn't until he took a class from the late bonsai artist Harold Lenz that he really became involved. "It's been all down hill ever since," Ivan said. "Each year its more and more bonsai with less and less time for anything else." Ivan's collection, which he describes as "too large," includes a wide variety of styles, sizes and material with a preference for pine and spruce. He has studied with a variety of bonsai masters including a 1986 study tour of Japan with American master Toshio Saburomaru. He is an active member and participant in half a dozen bonsai organizations. "Bonsai is an outlet for my artistic and creative abilities. It helps to reduce tension from my high stress profession, publishing, and provides me with an opportunity to share knowledge with others." Ivan has taught bonsai for the past six years. He presently conducts classes and demonstrations for Chicago's Field Museum, the Buddhist Temple of Chicago, the Morton Arboretum and at local garden centers. "A truly great bonsai can be felt. If the tree brings a positive emotional or strong spiritual experience to the viewer, then it's got to be great bonsai."

Scotch Pine
Pinus sylvestris

This specimen is an excellent example of the informal upright style of bonsai. The tree is 20 years old and has been in training for 10. It stands 45 in. high and is planted in an unglazed brown rectangular container of Japanese manufacture. The pine was pruned in the ground for three years and then moved to a training box for two years before being transferred to this finished container. It displays the classical, triangular silhouette seen in all outstanding bonsai. Scotch Pine make excellent bonsai specimens because of their exceptionally short needles and interesting bark patterns. This particular example also displays a gradually tapering trunk and excellent root placement setting it apart from others of its kind.

The Artist: Roland Folse, M.D.
Dr. Roland Folse is a practicing surgeon who first became acquainted with bonsai in the Seattle, Washington, area in 1962. He was inspired by the trees growing in the Cascade Mountains, as well as by such talented Puget Sound bonsai artists as Connie Raphael, Bert Brunner and Dan Robinson. He is an avid collector, and even after moving to central Illinois in 1971 still continues to collect bonsai material from the wild, especially in southern Texas. His collection is large and varied with 200 finished trees and another 500 or more in various stages of training. Dr. Folse is a self-taught bonsai artist who places strong emphasis on artistic attention to design and detail. He operates a small sideline bonsai business and both teaches and demonstrates bonsai locally. He is a former director of the American Bonsai Society and an active participant in Bonsai Clubs International, the Springfield Bonsai Society and the Midwest Bonsai Society. He has made a special study of propagation by cuttings and pine grafting and has a special interest in plants which grow in tropical or arid locations.

Chinese Sweet Plum
Sageretia theezans

It is unusual to find a Chinese Sweet Plum which exhibits the overall excellence seen in this fine, 10-year-old specimen. Its outstanding trunk taper and remarkably balanced root buttress are enhanced by the careful attention the artist has given to branch placement, balance and overall shape. This masterpiece bonsai stands 13 in. high and is planted in a shallow, blue glazed oval which accents the unique, two-toned coloring of the bark. The plant was purchased as a cutting 10 years ago and for the first five years was grown in the ground during summer months and potted each fall for storage in a greenhouse. Rough styling was accomplished during this time. It has been container grown for the past five years to permit detail styling. The wooden stand upon which the bonsai sits was hand-made by the artist.

The Artist: William M. Clark, M.D.

Dr. Bill Clark is a self-taught bonsai artist who developed his interest after viewing the Brooklyn Botanical Gardens Bonsai collection while living in New York in 1960. Today, Dr. Clark practices neurology in Tennessee and operates a "small time", back yard, bonsai business with his partner Hilda Kilgore. He has a particular fondness for maples, sweet plum and serissa, although his collection of more than 200 plants contains a wide variety of material. He has very few large bonsai and no two-man (very large) bonsai and does limited collecting. He is a past president and officer of the American Bonsai Society and a co-founder and president of the Nashville Bonsai Society for more than seven years. Dr. Clark notes that he has never purchased a finished bonsai, only uncut material which could be converted into bonsai. He is particularly adept at growing material from seed or cuttings and specializes in in-ground development to permit trunk enhancement. "Bonsai is a continuing artistic process. I find that very satisfying and relaxing."

Dwarf Hinoki Cypress
Chamaecyparis obtusa 'Nana'

This 60-plus year old, formal, upright bonsai was selected from a group of 50 balled and burlapped nursery plants in the summer of 1972. It was kept in a tub of sand, the roots undisturbed until the spring of 1973 when it was potted and styled. Hinoki is a much sought after subject for bonsai and this particular specimen is a superb example. It has been in training for 15 years and exhibits excellent branch placement and silhouette. The Hinoki's brilliant green foliage contrasts well with the reddish, exfoliating bark. It shows good root placement and a heavy tapering trunk which contributes to the bonsai's feeling of age and mass. The tree measures 36 in. high and is planted in a shallow 27 in. wide, gray, oval container of Japanese manufacture.

The Artist: M. Peter Voynovich

Chicago's Peter Voynovich became involved in bonsai in 1972. He has studied with masters such as John Naka, Toshio Saburomaru and Japan's Susumu Nakamura. Peter is a professional photographer who operates a color separation business in Chicago and is responsible for virtually all of the photographs used in this book. His well trained photographic eye has served him well in the design of his bonsai. Although his collection is quite small by most standards, only about 20 finished trees, all are excellent examples of his talent. He is an active participant and a past president of the Midwest Bonsai Society and has won two Best of Show titles and one Award of Merit for bonsai which he has exhibited at Midwest shows. There are many elements which go into the making of a good bonsai according to Peter. "I find it a very peaceful, relaxing and gratifying endeavor," he said.

Dwarf Japanese Garden Juniper
Juniperus procumbens 'Nana'

Japanese Garden Junipers are one of the most favored of all bonsai subjects. It is the material upon which most beginners are trained and from which many of the world's best bonsai are created. This excellent, informal, upright specimen not only speaks well of the artist's abilities, but amply displays why the species is so sought after as a bonsai subject. The planting began as a small cutting. It was field grown for 10 years and then placed in a growing container for an additional two years. It is approximately 20 years old and has been in training as a bonsai for the last four years. The artist has made dramatic use of deadwood, jin and shari, along the trunk line, causing it to sweep up and above the living portion of the plant. It is reminiscent of trees growing along a mountain timberline. The plant's gray, flaking bark contrasts nicely with the dense, green foliage of the Juniper. The bonsai stands 40 in. high and is planted in a brick-red, oval container made by the Sen-Ko-En pottery in Japan.

The Artist: F. Chase Rosade

Pennsylvania's Chase Rosade is one of America's premier bonsai artists. He encountered his first bonsai in the 1950s and by 1963 was completely "hooked." He then traveled to Japan to study with Master Kyzo Yoshida and by 1970 was operating a part-time bonsai business which quickly grew into Rosade Bonsai Studio, a full time labor of love. Today, Chase's talents are in high demand, and his studio, located in the rolling hills of Bucks County, Pennsylvania, offers a year round curriculum of classes and workshops as well as one of the most extensive collections of bonsai containers and plant material in the U.S. His large personal bonsai collection is both varied and breathtaking and his commercial bonsai operation among the biggest in the nation. His reputation as an experienced and gifted teacher keeps him on a rigorous lecture and demonstration schedule in the U.S. and abroad. He is an active member of many local and national bonsai organizations and consistently appears as a speaker or workshop leader at major bonsai conventions. "Bonsai has been and continues to be a way of life with me," Rosade said. "When I work on trees, the world stops."

Shimpaku Juniper
Juniperus chinensis 'Sargentii' 'Shimpaku'

This Sargents Juniper is an outstanding example of a semi-cascade style bonsai. The material is well developed and displays good balance. The bonsai is 12 years old and was grown from a rooted cutting. It has been in training for 10 years. It is planted in a brown Tokoname ware container from the Yamaaki Kiln in Japan. It stands 8 in. high and 24 in. wide.

The Artist: Joseph L. Noga

Joe Noga was an avid gardener and horticulturist for many years before taking his first bonsai class in 1977. Today he has an extensive collection which includes many smaller "shohin" class trees as well as a sizeable collection of large bonsai. He places a special emphasis on those varieties of plant material which can be grown in the northeastern U.S., but also enjoys growing maples, azaleas and dwarf pomegranates. Mr. Noga is a long-time student of nationally known bonsai teacher William Valavanis and has displayed his bonsai often at shows in the Midwest and upstate New York. He is a past president and active member of the Bonsai Society of Upstate New York and is a professor of Printing Management and Science at the Rochester Institute of Technology. "In addition to being an excellent form of relaxation, bonsai challenges your creativity and stimulates a stronger interest in horticulture," he said.

Buttonwood
Conocarpus erectus

Buttonwood is one of the most dramatic of all bonsai subjects due to the plant's natural tendency to develop large, dramatic areas of dead wood. The areas of dead wood, jin and shari, are fully evident on this exceptional specimen. They accentuate and enhance the informal upright styling of the plant and create the illusion of an ancient bonsai which has endured extreme hardship. Buttonwoods are extremely temperature sensitive and require large amounts of water to maintain good growth. For this reason they are found almost exclusively in the extreme southern reaches of Florida. This healthy and vigorous bonsai is a tribute not only to the talent of the artist, but to her horticultural expertise as well. The plant's actual age is unknown. It was collected in the lower Florida keys and has been in training as a bonsai for the past 11 years. It measures 34 in. tall and is planted in a dark brown, round container.

The Artist: Mary Madison

The pioneering work done with this species by Florida's Mary Madison has earned her the informal title of "buttonwood queen" in the American bonsai community. Her extensive collection is comprised almost entirely of collected material with a heavy emphasis on trees native to southern Florida, most notably Buttonwood. In 1978 one of her exceptional Buttonwood bonsai was officially named "Sen Ryu" or "Thousand Dragons" by the Meigo Kai bonsai group in Japan. It was the ninth tree ever named in the U.S. and she is the first woman to ever have been so honored. Mary has been interested in plants since she was a young child. As she grew older she developed an interest in art, and when she finally combined the two it came out bonsai. She has studied extensively with American masters John Naka and Ben Oki and is an avid student who takes all the workshops she can "get her hands on." Mary is a member of the Nippon Bonsai Society and a director of both the American Bonsai Society and Bonsai Societies of Florida. "I enjoy creating beautiful living things," she said, "but bonsai also helps to keep my mind in order."

California Juniper
Juniperus californica

California Junipers are highly prized as one of the most desirable and sought after species for training as bonsai. One glance at this excellent multiple trunk bonsai and this interest becomes obvious. Even before styling, California Junipers exhibit a rugged, weather beaten appearance. With even a little training they become miniature pictures of the forest giants. This specimen is a most recent addition to the artist's collection. It has been in training for only four years, having been purchased as partially trained stock from bonsai artist Merle Vanderwerd, who collected it in California. The bonsai is estimated to be more than 530 years old and stands over 44 in. high. It is planted in an unglazed, brown, oval container of Japanese manufacture. The large quantities of dead wood occur naturally on this species and add considerable drama to the overall design.

The Artist: **Arthur Cook**
Art Cook's involvement with bonsai began in 1978 when he joined the Minnesota Bonsai Society. Although he now lives in Las Vegas where he founded the Bonsai Society of Nevada, he still maintains his Minnesota membership as well as being active in several other regional and national bonsai organizations. He operates a commercial bonsai business in Las Vegas selling plant material, containers and other bonsai supplies and also maintains a personal collection numbering more than 350 trees, all of which he says are "still in training." Mr. Cook has studied with a variety of American masters including John Naka, Toshio Saburomaru and Keith B. Scott. "Beyond the obvious need for the skills of a talented artist, I believe that truly great stock is the key to a truly great bonsai," he said. "That's why I am an avid collector. The bonsaist hasn't been born who can do as good a job as mother nature."

Japanese Black Pine
Pinus thunbergii

This ancient, Japanese Black Pine is one of the oldest and most venerated bonsai in the America today. It is estimated to be more than 375 years old and first came to the United States in 1915 as one of several bonsai sent from Japan for display at the 1915 Pan Pacific Exposition held in San Francisco. This tree, like many others, disappeared into private collections after the Exposition. It was acquired by the artist and has been under his care for the past 30 years. It is an informal, upright style bonsai standing 37 in. tall and 46 in. wide. It is planted in an unglazed, brown, rectangular, Tokoname ware container which is traditionally used for pines of this type. The tree has flourished under the owner's care. Fine branch ramifications and consistently short needle length testify to hours of careful attention to detail by the artist. The tree displays a beauty and strength which can only be achieved through years of careful development. Throughout the world, black pines are sought after as bonsai subjects. Their interesting bark patterns and brilliant needles combine with the plant's tendency to bud back along old wood and to reduce its needle length, thus making it an excellent subject for bonsai.

The Artist: Mas Imazumi

Mas Imazumi was born in Oakland, California, but spent his early years in Japan. He returned to the U.S. just before the outbreak of World War II and spent more than four years in the Army. He is a professional landscape gardener and studied bonsai under the late master Homei Iseyama for many years. Within three years Iseyama recognized Imazumi's talent and began encouraging him to do public demonstrations. Mas Imazumi is one of a handful of exceptionally talented Japanese Americans living on the West Coast to whom the North American bonsai community owes a great debt. He and others like him, trained in the traditional Japanese methods, displayed an early willingness to share their knowledge with others. This openness did much to stimulate interest in bonsai throughout North America. Mas is a member of and instructor for several bonsai organizations in the San Francisco Bay area and is a past president of Fuji Bonsai, the second oldest bonsai club in North America. His personal collection is small, about 50 trees in a variety of styles. He prefers working with collected material and has a special preference for cascade style bonsai. "The difference between a good bonsai and a great bonsai is a feeling which comes from the recognition that the tree was created by an artist who was inspired by his material and was able to bring out its full beauty," he said.

EDITOR'S NOTE: I have included two photographs of Mas Imazumi's exceptional Japanese Black Pine. When the tree arrived in Minneapolis for the National Bonsai Foundation exhibit in July 1987, it looked like the photo on this page. Mr. Susumu Nakamura of Yokohama, an internationally known Japanese Bonsai master, was a featured speaker at the convention. Mr. Imazumi invited him to work on the tree and to thin branches to make room for later development. The result of Mr. Nakamura's efforts can be seen in the photograph on page 8.

_____ Bonsai #26

Lantana
Lantana

This excellent slant style bonsai was found growing on the lot where the artist built his present home in 1959. The tractor clearing the lot pulled it out of the ground. The artist salvaged the plant and trained it to the present shape. Actual age of the material is unknown; it has been in training for 28 years. The excellent branch ramifications indicate extensive pinching by the artist. The mounded soil mass, moss and subtle use of rocks act to counterbalance the tree's right-flowing motion. The bonsai stands 23 in. high and is planted in a round, handmade, gray glazed container.

The Artist: James J. Smith

In 1950 Florida's Jim Smith answered an advertisement in *Good Housekeeping* which told him he could "Learn the secrets of the oriental art of bonsai." "I sent in my ten bucks and have been learning ever since," he remarked. Smith retired from the construction business in Indiana in 1979 and moved to Vero Beach, Florida, where he now operates a wholesale bonsai business. His personal collection includes over 100 finished bonsai ranging in size from miniature to 4 ft. high. He specializes in tropical bonsai and has a particular interest in figs. Mr. Smith is an active participant on the Florida bonsai scene and frequently attends meetings at the national level. He has studied with a variety of American masters. "I have dedicated most of my adult life to bonsai and get a great deal of enjoyment in sharing my experiences with others, particularly beginner bonsai students." In his spare time he also makes his own stoneware bonsai pots.

74

San Jose Juniper
Juniperus san jose

This excellent, informal, upright bonsai is 32 years old and has been in training all its life. The plant was grown from a seedling by Kiyoko Hatanaka of California and purchased by the artist in 1982 when it was 27 years old. Considerable work has been done on the top third of the planting. Additional branches have been opened and repositioned and more areas of dead wood created. The tree was repotted into the present oval container in 1984. This container measures 17 in. wide and is a signed, Tokoname ware pot with a hand-rubbed, plum finish. Excellent root buttress, shape, taper and attention to detail all earmark this as an excellent bonsai, but its most appealing characteristic may be the many areas of deadwood, jin and shari, which appear throughout the planting and add a visual spark which keeps the viewer interested in examining the detail of each individual branch. The bonsai stands 25 in. high and 28 in. wide.

The Artist: William C. Smith
General William C. Smith was first exposed to bonsai during a tour of duty in Japan with the Air Force in 1960. For the next decade he read every book on bonsai he could find, but it wasn't until 1970 that his busy schedule allowed him to create his first tree. After 37 years of service, he is now retired and focuses most of his interest and energy on bonsai. "It has become more than a hobby for me," he said. "I spend five or six hours each day with my bonsai and derive a tremendous amount of peace and satisfaction by caring for them." General Smith's wife Robbieanna is equally as involved. Together they maintain a collection of more than 150 bonsai in various stages of training. Gen. Smith works with a variety of plant material, but has a special preference for pines. He is a member of several local and national bonsai organizations and has studied with numerous American Bonsai teachers, including Vaughn Banting, Warren Hill, Harry Hirao, John Naka, Ben Oki and Chase Rosade. "My bonsai teach me patience as well as giving me a sense of calmness and peace."

Smooth Leaf Elm
Ulmus carpinifolia

This informal, upright bonsai is an excellent example of the twin trunk style often referred to as "parent and child." The container is 2 in. deep and 28 in. wide, made by Yama Aki Kilns in Japan and originally owned by Toshio Kawamoto. The artist's decision to position the bonsai at the extreme right of the container, counterbalanced with a small stone positioned just to the left of center, creates a dramatic and exciting effect that would have been impossible to achieve had the bonsai been planted in a more traditional manner. The tree's light gray bark contrasts pleasantly with its dark green foliage. In addition, it displays an excellent root buttress and the fine twigging and branch ramification which indicate years of careful attention by its owner. The tree is 15 years old and was collected from the Chagrin River Valley in Ohio. It has been in training as a bonsai for the past seven years and stands 28 in. high.

The Artist: **Keith B. Scott**
Keith Scott of Chagrin Falls, Ohio, is a bonsai artist of remarkable skill. His excellent collection of more than 200 finished bonsai comprise only part of Mr. Scott's extensive bonsai garden and nursery known as Misago-En, located near Cleveland. He is an able teacher and lecturer who dispenses a measure of wit in combination with his bonsai wisdom. Mr. Scott is a well known national teacher of and writer on bonsai and has served as an officer or director for Bonsai Clubs International, The American Bonsai Society and the National Bonsai Foundation. Keith became involved with bonsai in 1938 and has studied with such well known masters as John Naka, Toshio Saburomaru, Yuji Yoshimura and Toshio Kawamoto. He has won numerous awards for his bonsai and in 1984 was asked to produce a one-man show for the Cleveland Museum of Natural History. He believes that consistency of form, style and material are the keys to outstanding bonsai. "I thrill in developing a beautiful tree from the commonplace; in short, making something from nothing, art from something common; the more common the better," he said.

Dwarf Japanese Garden Juniper
Juniperus procumbens 'Nana'

Japanese Garden Junipers are one of the most common subjects for bonsai, partially due to their ability to recover quickly and so forgive mistakes and partially because of their compact, luxuriant foliage and prostrate, growing habit. The Japanese Garden Juniper is an exceptionally hardy plant which does well in almost all climatic zones and actually seems to enjoy cultivation in a container. This specimen is approximately 25 years old and was obtained eight years ago as untrained, 5-gallon nursery stock. The top half of the tree was a prostrate branch which was moved 180 degrees to create the bonsai's new apex. Although it is styled as an informal upright, this bonsai exhibits a rhythmic harmony which suggests the flowing movement of a waterfall, a feeling which is most usually captured in cascade style bonsai. The tree stands 28 in. high and is planted in a red, unglazed oval container based on a Chinese design.

The Artist: Randy T. Clark
Randy Clark's involvement with bonsai began as a passing interest in the mid-1970s and has gradually grown into a condition he now describes as "chronic, compulsive tree trimming." With the help of his wife Nancy, he maintains an extensive collection of more than 300 bonsai in the garden of their Minneapolis home. Mr. Clark currently serves as a vice president of the National Bonsai Foundation and is active in a variety of other local and national bonsai organizations. In 1987 he formed White Dragon Bonsai Studio which offers educational programs and bonsai supplies for local residents. He is a frequent contributor to various national bonsai publications and was a featured speaker at the 1986 International Bonsai Congress in Washington D.C. In addition, he teaches bonsai locally for a variety of organizations including The Science Museum of Minnesota and the Minnesota State Horticultural Society. He has studied with a variety of bonsai masters, but ranks Toshio Saburomaru, John Naka and Chase Rosade as those who contributed most strongly to his bonsai education. "From Tosh I learned patience; from John the need to listen to what my trees say and from Chase the courage to be different," he said. "On the surface a bonsai is nothing more than a plant in a pot, but at its heart, a truly great bonsai is a strong emotional statement about its creator and about the way that person sees the whole of nature. Bonsai is a universal language which everyone understands."

Banyan or Willow Leaf Fig
Ficus neriifolia 'Regularis'

This clump or multiple trunk style bonsai is more than 30 years old and was originally obtained as neglected nursery stock which had been grown from a cutting in a 3-gallon container. The planting stands 25 in. high and 33 in. wide and has been in training as bonsai for 15 years. An excellent variety of trunk diameters contribute to this bonsai's feeling of mass and age. This particular *Ficus* cultivar grows vigorously, so the excellent layering of the foliage indicates the artist's careful attention to detail. The brown, unglazed Tokonoma ware container is a signed product of the Yamaka kiln. It's shallow, oval appearance contribute greatly to the bonsai's feeling of strength.

The Artist: Helen C. Souder

Florida's Helen Souder has been involved with bonsai since the early 1970s. She has studied with many American masters including John Naka, Chase Rosade and Yuji Yoshimura and has repeatedly accompanied Mr. Naka on tours of many of the great bonsai collections in Japan and elsewhere in the Orient. Ms. Souder's collection includes more than 135 plants in various stages of development. Due to her geographical location, many are tropical or semi-tropical species. She is an active member of several local and national bonsai organizations and teaches the art throughout southern Florida. She has been a featured speaker at Bonsai Societies of Florida and Bonsai Clubs International conventions, as well as an importer and wholesaler of bonsai pots and tools for many years. She was recently given a lifetime honorary membership in Florida's Lighthouse and Gold Coast Bonsai Societies for her contribution to the art. "I lose all sense of time when I create a bonsai," she said. "It gives a sense of satisfaction to work on them and to create something so pleasing when you are finished."

EDITOR'S NOTE: All five of the following bonsai were created by artist Jack Wikle of Michigan. Mr. Wikle has pioneered techniques for growing miniature bonsai continuously indoors under cool-white, fluorescent lighting. The specimens illustrated are examples of this growing technique as well as a testament to Mr. Wikle's considerable artistic abilities.

Bonsai # 31A

Dwarf Japanese Garden Juniper
Juniperus procumbens 'Nana'

An excellent miniature or shohin class bonsai in the cascade style. The tree is 10 years old and was grown from a rooted cutting. It measures 3¼ in. high and 4 in. wide and is planted in a square, gray, glazed cascade container. A common belief is that junipers will not survive indoors. This outstanding miniature bonsai is living proof that junipers can actually flourish indoors when properly grown. (See close-up page 87.)

Bonsai #31B

Dwarf Greek Myrtle
Myrtus communis 'Compacta'

A miniature bonsai styled in the informal, upright manner. The material is 11 years old, grown from a rooted cutting which the artist once planned to discard as unsuitable for bonsai. It stands 7 in. tall and is planted in a light blue, glazed, rectangular container.

Bonsai #31C

Littleleaf Cotoneaster
Cotoneaster microphylla

A semi-cascade style, shohin bonsai which was grown from a rooted cutting. It is eight years old and has been in training for five years. It is planted in a round, gray-glazed container created by bonsai artist and potter Sharon Muth. (See close-up page 87).

Beginning at the top of the photograph and going down: 31A Dwarf Japanese Garden Juniper; 31E Kingsville Boxwood; 31B Greek Myrtle; 31D Snow Rose; 31C Littleleaf Cotoneaster.

Snow-rose
Serissa foetida 'Double'

This modified broomstyle bonsai was given to the artist as a gift in 1976. It is 11 years old and has been in training as a bonsai for 10 years. The tree is 5 in. high and is planted in a dark blue, glazed, rectangular tray.

Kingsville Boxwood
Buxus microphylla 'Kingsville'

A modified broom style shohin grown from a rooted cutting. The bonsai is 10 years old and is planted on an unglazed, gray clay slab of Japanese manufacture. The bonsai stands 5 in. high.

The Artist: Jack Wikle

Jack Wikle of Tecumseh, Michigan, is an accomplished bonsai artist and writer with more than 20 years of experience growing outdoor bonsai. He has received most recognition, however, for his pioneering efforts in the design and cultivation of miniature bonsai, indoors under cool-white, fluorescent lighting. He travels and lectures on the techniques he has developed and frequently exhibits his superb, miniature bonsai at shows throughout the upper Midwest. In addition to the 55 shohin bonsai he grows under lights, his collection includes more than 80 which are grown outdoors in the traditional manner. He is the current editor of the *Journal of the American Bonsai Society* and a member of several local and national bonsai organizations. "Beyond the obvious attractions of form and color, I react to trees as symbols of the most basic elements of life and the natural world," he said. "Change and continuity, diversity and uniformity, force and counter force, all inextricably interlinked. My bonsai are an extension of my personality. They are a means of communicating my personal perceptions and feelings; a fulfillment of needs to explore myself and the world around me; to innovate, to create and nurture . . . and also a quiet escape. In short, I have responded to a need to help trees grow and discovered in the process the trees are helping me to grow."

Littleleaf Cotoneaster

Japanese Garden Juniper

Mugho Pine
Pinus mugo 'Mugo'

This classical, formal upright style bonsai is all the more exciting due to the species from which it was styled. Mugho pines, because of their small needle size and willing tendency to "bud back," make excellent subjects for bonsai. However, because of the plant's natural tendency towards spreading growth, they are usually styled as informal uprights or cascades and almost never as a formal upright. In this case the talented hand of one of America's foremost teachers has created an exceptional, formal, upright bonsai. The tree is more than 34 years old and has been in training for 32 years. It is one of the first bonsai ever created by the artist and was the only single upright trunk among a large number of one-gallon specimens from which the artist had to select. The tree measures 22 in. tall and is planted in an unglazed, brown, rectangular container of Japanese manufacture. It exhibits the triangular silhouette, correct branch placement and excellent root buttress and trunk taper required to mark it as truly classical, formal, upright bonsai.

The Artist: Toshio Saburomaru
The name Saburomaru ranks with those of such important figures as Naka and Yoshimura in terms of their fundamental contribution to the development of bonsai on this continent. This is true not only of Tosh's considerable artistic talent, but also his consistent willingness to share his talent and knowledge with others. Tosh was born in Hollister, California, but returned to Japan at the age of 10. In the following 10 years he developed a love for Japan's natural landscapes which lead him to study not only bonsai, but many of Japan's other arts including painting, haiku poetry and landscape gardening. Upon his return to the U.S., he served the Army for five years, after which he opened a landscaping business while continuing to work with bonsai. By 1950 the demand for his bonsai skills had drawn him into teaching the art. Word of his talent as a teacher spread quickly and today Tosh is a much-sought-after bonsai master who travels extensively throughout Canada, the U.S. and Latin America teaching and demonstrating the art of bonsai. He continues to run his landscaping business near San Francisco with his oldest son, Robert, and also operates a bonsai nursery which sells plant material, tools, pots and other supplies. Tosh's personal bonsai collection includes over 300 trees collected from around the country, many of which were started as seedlings collected more than 35 years ago. Mr. Saburomaru is also one of the founding members of Bonsai Clubs International and frequently leads tours of many of the famous bonsai gardens and collections in Japan.

Dwarf Hinoki Cypress
Chamaecyparis obtusa 'Nana'

Formal upright is the basic form from which all other styles of bonsai proceed. The essential simplicity of the design makes it a difficult style to execute effectively. Branch placement, shape and proportion are more critical here than in any other style. This splendid Hinoki Cypress attests to the artist's clear understanding of those requirements. The trees displays an excellent root buttress and gradual trunk taper, highlighted by correct branch placement, creating the classical triangular silhouette of an outstanding, formal, upright bonsai. The tree is 25 years old and was obtained from 15 year old, field grown nursery stock. It was originally styled as a demonstration piece at the International Bonsai Symposium held in Rochester, New York, in September 1984. It stands 36 in. tall and is planted in a glazed, turquoise container.

The Artist: Lynn K. Porter

Lynn K. Porter of Philadelphia became involved in bonsai in the mid-1960s as a student of Chase Rosade. Her part-time interest quickly became a full time vocation, and today she serves as an associate with Rosade Bonsai Studio. She is a talented bonsai artist who has traveled extensively throughout Japan and studied with such Japanese masters as Susumo Sudo and Mikio Oshima. Ms. Porter is an active participant on the local and national bonsai scene and has written numerous articles for various national bonsai publications. She maintains a large, diverse collection of bonsai at the Studio in New Hope, Pennsylvania, which she describes simply as "all types" and "too many." "Bonsai is a great creative outlet," she said. "Much better than cooking." She is particularly adept at field growing stock material for later training as bonsai. "I enjoy watching them develop and then wiring and potting them." "It's a great culmination to many years of work."

Kashima Japanese Maple
Acer palmatum 'Kashima'

The Kashima Japanese Maple is a dwarf cultivar belonging to the "yatsub-usa" or multiple-bud grouping of ornamental plant material. This specimen is a truly remarkable accomplishment and is typical of the excellence in bonsai design which is a trademark of this artist. It is an informal, upright style bonsai standing 26 in. high and was grown from a 5 in. long, pencil-sized cutting. The tree was used as a stock plant for six years before the artist decided to train it as a bonsai. The tree is 17 years old and planted in a British, contemporary oval, cream glaze container by potter Gordon Duffett. Extremely fine twigging contribute to the lush feeling and the well rounded silhouette of the bonsai. Its root buttress is well proportioned and the plant's taper, balance and harmony with its container are in the best classical style.

The Artist: William N. Valavanis

Bill Valavanis is one of the leading figures in American bonsai. His involvement began at the early age of 11 and has grown to establish him as a recognized expert in the art. He is a classical bonsai artist whose favorite plant materials include a wide variety of pines and maples plus many other unusual and hard to find species. Mr. Valavanis has studied with Japanese American master Yuji Yoshimura as well as with such Japanese masters as Kyuzo Murata, Kakutaro Komuro, Toshio Kawamoto, Tameji Nakajima and Mikio Oshima. He is the editor and publisher of *International Bonsai Magazine,* the finest English language publication on bonsai in the world, and the founder and owner of The International Bonsai Arboretum in Rochester, New York. He is a much-sought-after teacher and lecturer and has traveled extensively throughout the U.S., Canada, England and Australia teaching bonsai. He is active in a variety of local and national bonsai organizations and a frequent speaker and demonstrator at national conventions. "I enjoy expressing myself through nature," he said.

Sierra Juniper
Juniperus occidentalis

This tree is approximately 350 years old and has been in training for 15 years. It is styled in the informal upright or curving trunk style and stands 32½ in. high. It is planted in a rectangular container made of unglazed, dark brown clay. The bonsai was collected in the Sierra Nevada mountains of the western United States and is particularly noteworthy because of its excellent root buttress, gradual taper and dramatic use of jin and shari.

The Artist: Hiroshi Suzuki

"Great bonsai . . . like beauty, is in the eye of the beholder," according to Hiroshi Suzuki, who was aware of that beauty as a boy growing up in Japan. However, it was not until he immigrated into the U.S. in 1960 that he became seriously involved in the art. "Bonsai is a form of meditation and therapy," he said. "It is a way to relax and to reduce stress and tension." Mr. Suzuki's collection includes more than 50 specimens mostly of Black Pine and Sierra Juniper. In addition, he is a member of and instructor for the San Francisco Bay Bonsai Club and also maintains a large bonsai collection for the Kyoto Koi and Garden Center in Santa Rosa, California.

Rocky Mountain Juniper
Juniperus scopulorum

This excellent, collected specimen is estimated to be over 200 years old and has been in training as a bonsai for 11 years. It was originally planted in a 3 ft. long box to accommodate a large main root. Five years were required to reduce the length of this root and develop fine feeder roots which would allow the plant to be safely transplanted into its present 15 in. wide by 3½ in. deep, round, brown container. The planting originally had four trunks. One was removed in May 1987 creating the present tree and a new single trunk driftwood style bonsai (not pictured). The bonsai measures 32 in. high and features a dramatic show of deadwood, jin and shari, which is typical of collected plant material from the higher elevations of the Rocky Mountains.

The Artist: James T. Robinson
Colorado's Jim Robinson attended a Los Angeles bonsai show in 1961 and has been creating his own bonsai ever since. His collection presently numbers over 120 plants in various stages of styling. "I love them all," he said, "but I have a special interest in root-over-rock and cascade style bonsai." Robinson is a past president of the Rocky Mountain Bonsai Society and has studied with such local bonsai experts as the late Bob Kataoka and Kai Kawahara. "Bonsai is a challenge both intellectually and aesthetically. I am especially fond of 3-dimensional art and bonsai is the best."

Shimpaku Juniper
Juniperus chinensis 'Sargentii' 'Shimpaku'

Twenty three years ago this bonsai began as a three-year-old San Jose Juniper planted in a one-gallon growing container. Gradually the gray-green, prickly San Jose foliage was replaced with grafts of lush and brilliant green 'Shimpaku' foliage. Four years later it was transferred to a bonsai container and has been in continuous training since. Styled as an informal upright, this bonsai measures 25 in. high and is planted in a gray, unglazed, rectangular container of Japanese manufacture. The tightness of the foliage and the virtual absence of grafting scars mark this bonsai as an outstanding technical achievement. The excellent silhouette, radial root placement and classical, informal, upright style mark it as an artistic achievement as well.

The Artist: Masaru Ishii

Mas Ishii opened his Chikugo-En Bonsai Nursery in Gardena, California in 1981. Since that time he has carved a unique niche for himself in bonsai history. His work in the grafting of the small 'kishu" variety of 'Shimpaku' foliage onto 'San Jose' stock has gained him a reputation throughout North America. Mas became involved in bonsai 22 years ago; today he is an active artist and professional grower who's personal collection numbers over 250 plants of varying types and sizes. He has a special preference for cascade, informal upright and bunjin styles. Although many of his bonsai are quite small (mame class) he also has several large collected California Junipers. His wife Reiko helps in his commercial nursery operation, which is tightly packed into a small lot beside a busy highway in western Los Angeles. The nursery's plants number in the thousands and include large numbers of the grafted Kishu Shimpaku for which he has become so famous. "I find it very relaxing to work on my bonsai, and it gives me great pleasure just to look at them," he said. Mas was a student of Harry Hamasaki and today teaches grafting and bonsai on his own. He is a member of seven national and local bonsai organizations.

Sierra Juniper
Juniperus occidentalis

This exceptional bonsai is an outstanding example of the twin trunk style. The areas of dead wood, jin and shari, are well considered and sweep sharply to the left. These striking features permit the bonsai to be planted at the extreme right side of a low, shallow container. The selection of jin and subsequent arrangement in container draws the viewer into the planting and creates an illusion of extreme age. The bonsai's actual age is unknown. The plant was collected six years ago growing between two large granite cracks in California's Sierra Nevada mountains. It has been in training for three years. The bonsai is 18 in. tall and is planted in a brown rectangular tray 25 in. wide. The survival rate for collected *Juniperus occidentalis* is very small, making this an even more valuable bonsai.

The Artist: Hideko Metaxas

San Francisco's Hideko Metaxas inherited her first bonsai as a Christmas present more than 15 years ago. Today, her collection numbers over 100 plants, although she claims that only about 30 are "really good." She has studied with a number of California bonsai artists including the late Bob Kato and is an active member in a host of bonsai organizations in California. "Great bonsai is made by the artist who captures the tree's natural beauty and emphasizes it to the maximum," she said. Her collection includes a variety of styles with a special preference for the free form or "bunjin" style of bonsai. In addition to lecturing and demonstrating bonsai for groups in the Bay area, she also teaches Ikebana and has an avid interest in calligraphy, ceramics, Japanese painting, and suiseki.

Japanese Hornbeam
Carpinus japonica

This excellent bonsai has been trained from a seedling for the last 15 years. It is styled as an informal, upright, root-over-rock bonsai, and displays an excellent silhouette and a remarkable root buttress. The bonsai measures 20 in. high and is planted in a dark blue, oval Tokoname ware container by Reiho. Excellent root-over-rock bonsai are difficult to create due to the time required in making the plant material grow in harmony with the rock effectively. This Hornbeam is a classic example and speaks of much diligence on the part of the artist.

The Artist: Harvey B. Carapella

Harvey Carpella of New York State is 44 years old and has been active with bonsai for the past 12 years. He works as a commercial illustrator and designer and finds bonsai offers a welcome change from his daily routine yet allows him to utilize his natural artistic abilities. Harvey believes the true difference between good and great bonsai is refinement. His work amply reflects this belief. His collection includes more than 80 plants in finished containers, exhibiting different levels of refinement, plus an additional 40 or more plants in various stages of training. He is an active member and past president of the Bonsai Society of Upstate New York and has studied with such well known teachers as William Valavanis and Toshio Saburomaru. "My only regret is that someone did not introduce me to bonsai when I was much younger," he said.

Bonsai #40

Common Pasture Juniper
Juniperus communis 'Depressa'

This excellent, slant style bonsai was designed from material collected in 1979. It is estimated to be 80 years old and has been in training for six years. The bonsai stands 21 in. high and is planted in a 12 in. square by 6 in. deep container with a textured gray finish. Although this species of juniper grows wild throughout much of North America, this specimen is particularly outstanding and received the Best of Show award at the 1985 Mid America Bonsai Exhibit in Chicago.

The Artist: Jack B. Douthitt

Wisconsin's Jack Douthitt started his horticultural career looking for exotic house plants in Chicago and by 1975 was one of the founders of the Badger Bonsai Society. His first bonsai, a Japanese Maple seedling purchased from a commercial bonsai nursery, has blossomed into an extensive collection comprised mostly of locally available material with a particular emphasis on the Wisconsin form of juniper used here. He is an architect who abandoned his interest in drawing and painting for bonsai. "Once a painting is finished, I lose my emotional involvement with it. In bonsai, the creative process never stops and the emotional involvement with it never ends," he said. "The process of creating a great bonsai starts with the ability to select material with outstanding potential. It then requires a design that utilizes the potential of that material. Finally, it is the ability of the artist to bring all of the elements of the design into a pleasing and unified whole. In bonsai . . . the whole is always greater than the sum of the parts."

Japanese Black Pine
Pinus thunbergii

Although this excellent, Black Pine specimen has been in training for more than 31 years its actual age is unknown. The artist purchased the plant at an auction in 1973 and restyled it shortly thereafter to become the logo tree for the American Bonsai Society. The tree was again restyled in 1977 to its present form and is an excellent example of the bunjin or literati (free form) style of bonsai. It measures 35 in. high and is planted in a 14 in. diameter drum pot. Although the primary focus of any bonsai is the tree, the clay composition of this unglazed container is particularly interesting because its dark brown color shows tints of reddish brown at the high points. It illustrates how important the selection of just the right container for a bonsai can be.

The Artist: Jack E. Billet

Jack Billet of Delaware first discovered bonsai in a 1967 *Reader's Digest* article but didn't become really involved until 1969 when he bought a copy of the Sunset book *Bonsai*. "It's been an out-and-out love affair ever since," he notes. Mr. Billet has studied the art in Japan with teachers such as Hiroyshi Oi and Koji Amakawa as well as with American masters Frank Okamura and John Naka. His collection is extensive and includes a wide variety of styles and plants in all stages of development, with a special preference for bunjin style bonsai. He is an active participant on both the local and national bonsai scene. Being able to relate to the tree is one of the most important elements in bonsai, according to Billet. "When you look at a bonsai you must be able to feel it . . . to look at it and know that you have been there. It is very satisfying to create a thing of beauty that you enjoy and then discover that others enjoy it as well," he said.

Cryptomeria
Cryptomeria japonica 'Tansu'

This Cryptomeria forest of 11 trees was produced from 12-year-old cuttings specially selected to complement the rugged stone. The short needles and tight growth habit of *Cryptomeria* help to maintain the excellent proportion throughout the planting. The California Aqua Stone on which the planting is made is narrow front and back. To increase the planting area two screen "pockets" were constructed and affixed onto the back of the rock so that these pockets are not detectable from the front. The planting measures 9½ in. high, 18½ in. wide and only 8 in. deep.

The Artist: Terry Ward
Terry Ward's involvement with bonsai began with a newspaper photograph in the early 1970s. Today, Mr. Ward operates Man Sui-En Bonsai Nursery in northern California. His personal collection contains a wide variety of plant material including deciduous, flowering and fruiting bonsai, as well as evergreen and needle trees ranging in size from under 1 in. to over 3 ft.He is active in five California bonsai organizations, one of which he founded, and is a former trustee of the Golden State Bonsai Federation. In addition to teaching bonsai, he has studied with such American masters as John Naka, Khan Komai, Mitsuo Umehara and the late Bob Kato. He sums up the essence of great bonsai in a single word . . . Harmony.

_____ Bonsai #43

Rocky Mountain Juniper
Juniperus scopulorum

This tree is approximately 250 years old, but has been in training as bonsai for only three years. It is a collected specimen from the 14,000-foot level of the Rocky Mountains near Estes Park, Colorado. It is styled as a formal upright and measures 24½ in. high. It has excellent taper and makes a dramatic use of areas of deadwood, jin and shari. The container in which it is planted is an unglazed, dark brown rectangle 13 in. wide of Japanese manufacture. The juniper was collected in the spring of 1984 and containerized in the spring of 1986.

The Artist: Allan Hills
Allan Hills is a geologist who became involved with bonsai in 1970 in Buffalo, New York. He lives and works in Colorado today and is adept at "bringing them back alive." "I love the thrill of the chase," he said, "of going out and searching for suitable trees." His collection numbers more than 100 trees ranging from cuttings to bonsai in training for the past 16 years. He is an active participant in local and national bonsai organizations and has taught introductory bonsai classes in Colorado for the last five years. "I get a great deal of satisfaction from designing something which I feel is beautiful. In addition I think the relaxation and enjoyment I get from working with my bonsai add quantity and quality to my life." According to Hills, a truly great bonsai is one in which the individual aspects of trunk, roots and crown all work together to create the desired illusion of scale.

110

Japanese Garden Juniper
Juniperus procumbens

This informal, upright style bonsai makes heavy use of dead wood along the trunk of the tree and in so doing creates a remarkable picture of strength, age and venerability. Japanese Garden Junipers are one of the most rewarding of all bonsai subjects, but this particular specimen was a unique find. It was one of several foundation plantings originally installed at D. Hill Nursery in Dundee, Illinois. The plantings had become overgrown and were about to be bulldozed when the artist happened along. The bonsai is approximately 85 years old and has been in training for seven years. It stands 34 in. high and is planted in a brown, unglazed, oval container of Japanese manufacture.

The Artist: Alex Alexander

Alex Alexander has now retired to his farm near Meredian, Mississippi, but for many years was one of the guiding forces for the development of bonsai in the upper Midwest. He is a professional botanist and horticulturist who developed an interest in bonsai while stationed in Japan after World War II. Mr. Alexander is a charter member of the Midwest Bonsai Society in Chicago and has served twice as its president. Over the years he has shaped and styled literally hundreds of bonsai although his personal collection contains only 30 or 40 trees. "I prefer to help other people in developing their collections," he said. "Many of the trees in the Midwest which are considered good, at one time or another started off in life as mine." In addition to his professional training in horticulture, Mr. Alexander has studied with a variety of masters including John Naka and for the past 10 years with Japan's Susumu Nakamura. Alex's bonsai have consistently won awards for their excellence at Midwest bonsai exhibition through the years. "I have had a lifelong interest in asymmetrical natural art forms. I guess I just like to help nature along in some artistic fashion."

Ponderosa Pine
Pinus ponderosa

This excellent, pine bonsai was naturally shaped into a free form style known as literati or bunjin. The artist collected the tree from the high elevations of the Rocky Mountains near Lyons, Colorado, where it was growing as a natural bunjin style. The tree was placed in a training container allowed to grow vigorously for three years, after which it was potted into its present round, unglazed container and "touched up" by the artist. The tree stands 30 in. high and is estimated to be more than 250 years old. It has been trained as a bonsai for 30 years. Collected pines and junipers from the high Rockies are greatly valued as bonsai. Judging from this specimen and others appearing in these pages, it is easy to understand why. The harsh conditions under which these trees survive for centuries create dramatic, ancient specimens which, as in this case, often only require minor interventions in shape or branch placement to bring out the inherent beauty of the plant. Literati style is not well understood and difficult to execute for most students. Not so in this case. The bonsai exhibits a free flowing trunk movement which is well balanced by the foliage mass. The movement thus created is visually fascinating to explore.

The Artist: Kai Kawahara
Colorado's Kai Kawahara was born in Japan. As a youth his father assigned him the job of watering the family bonsai. By the time he was 12 he had developed a fascination with the art and has continued his involvement for more than 56 years. His personal collection numbers more than 500 specimens including many collected Red, Ponderosa, Limber and Bristle Cone pines as well as juniper, fir, spruce and many types of azalea and Japanese plum. While growing up in Japan, Mr. Kawahara studied with master Tomoe Asayeda of Hiroshima. He has been honored for both his bonsai and his contributions to the art by the Japan Bonsai Society, the Denver Senior Bonsai Club and the Rocky Mountain Bonsai Society, of which he is an active member. "The best bonsai are formed naturally," he said. "It is difficult for man to duplicate the natural essence of a collected bonsai. To create a truly great tree you must feel it in very much the same way a musician feels his music. I'm not sure why I love bonsai so much. It relaxes me and I find a great deal of enjoyment in seeing plants grow. I do know that if it were removed from my life, I am sure I would perish."

EDITOR'S NOTE: By strict definition, this is not a bonsai at all. It is a Chinese Rock Penjing. Although the words bonsai and penjing have essentially the same meaning, it is evident that this Rock Penjing is very different from the other artworks illustrated in this book. I have included it because many North Americans, like the artist, are discovering a new interest in this ancient Chinese art form. I thought this one deserved to be seen and am certain more will be seen as the techniques for their construction become better known in North America.

Chinese Rock Penjing

The stones of this planting are arranged on a 36 in. wide, oval, marble tray. The tallest rock measures 24½ in. high. The white marble slab simulates the waters of a Chinese inland sea. The stones are planted with four- and five-year old seedlings of Japanese White Pine (*Pinus parvifloria*) and Kingsville Boxwood (*Buxus microphilla* 'Kingsville'). Unlike Japanese plantings, small ceramic figurines of people, bridges and temples are often a typical element in Chinese penjing, of which this excellent example is no exception. The scale of the planting is dramatic. The illusion of depth and the overall impact conveyed by the arrangement is like a large landscape painting and cannot be effectively captured on film.

The Artist: Hal Mahoney

Hal Mahoney became interested in Chinese penjing in 1982 when he encountered a number of them at a floral exhibition in Amsterdam, Holland. He has been involved with bonsai since 1972 and believes his interest in bonsai is a natural outgrowth of his training in the biological sciences. Hal is a past president of both the Long Island Bonsai Society and the Bonsai Society of Greater New York as well as a current board member of Bonsai Clubs International. His collection is composed of 45–50 bonsai which he considers suitable for display, plus an unknown number of plants in various stages of training. He is an amateur horticultural scientist and conducts a variety of plant experiments in the areas of propagation, air layering and grafting. Mahoney considers originality and skill vital ingredients in the creation of a truly unique bonsai masterpiece. In 1976 he introduced bonsai as a credit course in the Babylon Public School System and has been teaching beginning and advanced bonsai courses ever since. "I enjoy growing plants and being able to apply my artistic skills to create living works of art," he said. "There is a great feeling of accomplishment in being able to create something as beautiful and unique as a bonsai."

Catlin Elm
Ulmus parvifolia 'Catlin'

This excellent forest of Catlin Elms is planted on a coral slab obtained from the Florida Keys. The small stone inscribed with Japanese kanji says "Yu lin" or "Walk in the Woods," which is appropriate since this tiny planting truly creates the feeling of a wooded knoll on a warm summer day. Catlins are a particular favorite for bonsai because of their exceptionally small, dark green foliage. However, the Catlin cultivar is a sport or aberation of the Chinese Elm. The small, dark green leaves can only be maintained when propagated vegetatively by cutting or grafts. This planting of 15 trees was made four years ago from rooted cuttings grown by the artist for more than 12 years. During that time the plants have developed substantial trunks and excellent branch ramifications, which indicate careful attention to pruning and shaping. Careful placement of larger trunks in the foreground and smaller trunks in the back create a feeling of depth in the bonsai. The forest stands 14 in. tall and is 24 in. wide.

The Artist: Sigmund Dreilinger
Sig Dreilinger was a founding member of the Bonsai Society of Greater New York, but has since retired and moved to Florida. Thanks to his involvement with bonsai, he is now working harder than ever. He is a member of at least 10 local and national bonsai organizations and currently serves as president of Bonsai Clubs International. Until his retirement to Florida in 1982 he maintained an extensive collection of bonsai, many of which were donated to the Brooklyn and Queens Botanic Gardens. His personal collection now consists of approximately 40 tropical and semi-tropical bonsai. Sig's involvement with bonsai can be traced back to 1955. He has studied extensively with American teachers, such as Kan Yashiroda, Yuji Yoshimura and John Naka, and is a frequent contributor to various bonsai publications. "After 40 years, I am more involved in bonsai than ever before, and I seem to create my plantings with no consideration of how many years it may take them to become excellent specimens," he said. "The enjoyment of bonsai comes not only from the ability to create beauty and drama but also from the enjoyment of watching it grow and develop through the years."

Elephant Bush
Portulacaria afra

This charming, cascade bonsai is an excellent example of the suitability of tropical or semi-tropical plant material for styling as bonsai. Elephant Bush is a close relative of the Jade Plant (*Crassula argentea*), and as such does not readily respond to the bending and shaping of branches with wire. This specimen, however, has been effectively shaped into a two-line, cascade style bonsai. The plant material was obtained from a local greenhouse and is approximately seven years old. It has been in training for the past four years. According to the artist the plant had one very long lower branch and was styled based on a photograph appearing on page 158 of John Naka's book *Techniques I*. The tree is planted in a square, unglazed, brown, cascade container and stands 17 in. from top to tip of cascade.

The Artist: Ruth H. Delaney

Minnesota's "Buffy" Delaney is a relative newcomer to bonsai. Her involvement began in 1981 when her brother, also a bonsai artist, sent her a copy of the Brooklyn Botanical Garden's publication on indoor bonsai. Her collection is growing rapidly and currently includes about 50 specimens which she maintains "still need years and years and years of work." Most of Buffy's bonsai are trees hardy in Minnesota. However, because she has a small greenhouse, she has also developed an interest in tropical and semi-tropical species. Buffy is an active member of the local bonsai club and has studied with a number of American bonsai artists. "Bonsai is an art that is never finished," she said. "A tree can always be developed and refined even further, but the difference between good and great bonsai is the illusion that it has had a tremendous struggle against nature. Artistic sculpting of dead wood combined with compact, vigorous, live growth create a remarkable picture. When you can duplicate that look with common nursery stock it is a tremendous achievement."

Trident Maple
Acer buergerianum

This bonsai was dug from a landscape nursery in 1982 when it was 15–20 ft. tall. It now stands 36 in. high and has been in training for five years. It was planted in its present gray, oval, tokoname ware container two years ago. The Trident is estimated to be 30 years old and is affectionately referred to as "Big Bertha" by its owner. Most Trident Maple bonsai in the U.S. and Canada have been obtained as imports from Japan. This particular, informal, upright specimen is of note because it displays excellent trunk to apex taper and because it has been totally grown and developed in North America. Trident Maples are particularly sought after as bonsai subjects due to their small leaf size and to the plants tendency to "fuse" surface roots thus permitting the development of large and impressive root buttresses.

The Artist: Brussel Martin
Brussel Martin of Olive Branch, Mississippi, is a well known figure throughout the U.S. bonsai community. Together with his partner, Maury Strauss, he operates Brussel's Bonsai Nursery. His personal collection numbers only about 50 trees, but the nursery's specimens number in the thousands. For over a decade he has grown and imported quality bonsai stock as well as a full line of imported pots, tools, books and other bonsai accessories. Brussel has studied extensively in the U.S. and in Japan and is a director of Bonsai Clubs International. His first bonsai was acquired as a gift from his father at age eight. He describes bonsai as an art form like no other, always changing, always growing. "Great bonsai are rare because of the time it takes to develop really outstanding material," he said. "I don't think many people in the United States really understand what it takes to make a truly great bonsai."

Cedar Elm
Ulmus crassifolia

This multiple trunk bonsai was made from material collected in the Lake Belton area of Texas in 1981. It is estimated to be 50–60 years old and has been in training for six years. The tallest tree in the planting is 37 in. high and is planted in a unglazed, oval tray of Japanese manufacture. The composition is well balanced and exhibits a light, airy feeling.

The Artist: A. R. Hawkins
Archie Hawkins of Houston, Texas, developed his interest in bonsai after reading an article on the subject in the magazine *Better Homes and Gardens.* Shortly thereafter he began growing plants in boxes, wooden pots and anything else that would hold them. Five years ago he suffered a major setback when his collection was almost totally destroyed by several days of severe freezing weather in the Houston area. The Cedar Elm illustrated and one other were the only two which survived. Since that time he has slowly begun to rebuild his collection. He is a past president of the Houston Bonsai Society and a former director of the American Bonsai Society. "Bonsai fills both a physical and mental need for me," he said.

A multiple trunk Scotch Pine bonsai by Mike Hansen of Austin, Texas.

HOW TO FIND OUT MORE ABOUT BONSAI

If you are new to bonsai, then looking at the pictures in this book may have stimulated you to try your hand. Don't be afraid. Like any art form, bonsai is an acquired skill which continues to improve with practice. It is not difficult and a basic understanding of the fundamentals can be gained in just a few hours. With a little time and practice you can be on your way to creating your own masterpiece bonsai in just a few weeks.

You would probably like some help, however. Help is available. First I suggest you check the shelves of your local library or book store. You should find at least a modest selection of publications on the subject. I can personally recommend *Bonsai* by Deborah R. Koreshoff as an excellent book for beginners. It is published by Timber Press, 9999 S.W. Wilshire, Portland, Oregon 97225.

Secondly, find out if there are any bonsai clubs or organizations in your area, and if so, join. If not, then find some friends who are also interested in bonsai and form your own club. I suggest you check with your local university agricultural extension office or your local horticultural society. They usually have a current listing of the various flower and garden organizations in the area. There are well over 100 bonsai clubs throughout the U.S. and Canada with memberships which range from three to 300. If there are others around who are interested in bonsai then affiliate yourself with them. You will learn faster and make fewer mistakes if you share what you are learning with others.

The American Bonsai Society and Bonsai Clubs International are the two major bonsai organizations on this continent. Both produce excellent, English language magazines filled with informative articles on bonsai. In addition, the magazine's ads are a good way to find sources for the various bonsai supplies you will need such as pots, tools, soils etc. Both organizations hold national conventions each year and both organizations offer a lending library of books, slides programs and video tapes available to members for a nominal charge. I strongly urge your participation in either one or both of these organizations. Their addresses are:

American Bonsai Society
Box 358
Keene, NH 03431

Bonsai Clubs International
#277
2636 W. Mission Road
Tallahassee, FL 32304

A Trident Maple bonsai by Bob Hampel of Minnesota.

INDEX BY NAME OF ARTIST

INDEX BY BOTANICAL NAME
OF PLANT

Botanical Name	Common Name	Page Number
PINUS		
—*flexilis*	Limber Pine	44
—*mugo 'Mugo'*	Mugho Pine	88
—*parviflora*	Japanese White Pine	166
—*ponderosa*	Ponderosa Pine	42, 114
—*sylvestris*	Scotch Pine	58
—*thunbergii*	Japanese Black Pine	50, 72, 106
PLANERA		
—*aquatica*	Water Elm	26
PORTULACARIA		
—*afra*	Elephant Bush	120
SAGERETIA		
—*theezans*	Chinese Sweet Plum	60
SAMAN		
—*arboreum*	Rain Tree	36
SERISSA		
—*foetida 'Double'*	Snow Rose	86
SEQUOIA		
—*sempervirens*	Coast Redwood	32
THUJA		
—*occidentalis*	American Arborvitae	30, 54
ULMUS		
—*americana*	American Elm	50
—*carpinifolia*	Smooth Leaf Elm	78
—*crassifolia*	Cedar Elm	124
—*parvifolia 'Catlin'*	Catlin Elm	118

Everett